20TH *ZEN JURY*
Poems, Songs and Prayers

BILL O'BRIAN

Andrew Benzie Books
Pleasant Hill, California

Published by Andrew Benzie Books
www.andrewbenziebooks.com

Copyright © 2015 Bill O'Brian
All rights reserved. Except as permitted under the U.S. Copyright Act of 1976, no part of this publication may be reproduced, distributed or transmitted in any form or by any means, or stored in a database or retrieval system without prior written permission of the author.

Printed in the United States of America

First Edition: October 2015

10 9 8 7 6 5 4 3 2 1

O'Brian, Bill
20th Zen Jury: Poems, Songs and Prayers

ISBN: 978-1-941713-22-8

Cover and book design by Andrew Benzie

This book is dedicated to my sister Mary.

TABLE OF CONTENTS

POEMS
1. A Happy Day 1
2. Extensions of the Sun 2
3. Humans Being 3
4. Where You Stay 4
5. Inside as Usual 5
6. Matters in Between 6
7. Listen to the Spirit 7
8. Options/Actions 8
9. Be Here Now 9
10. Shorty 10
11. Unconscious Streams #1 11
12. Unconscious Streams #3 13
13. Unconscious Streams #4 15
14. Unconscious Streams #5 17
15. Proverbs 19
16. Mister Doctor Martin Luther King 20
17. To My Students 22
18. 1981 Re-Visited 23
19. Frequent Responses 25
20. Your Life Flowing 27
21. Another Moment in Time 29
22. Love is the Dream 31
23. Not a Word Between Them 32
24. Some Thoughts for Sheryl & Jerry 34
25. The Soulful Van Sings of Pain 36
26. Keeping Faith In Mind 37
27. Our Friend Indeed 38
28. From May to June 39
29. Golf on a Sunny Afternoon 40

30.	Summer's Here; Let's Cheer!	41
31.	Good to Go	42
32.	Christmas Eve	43
33.	Look Around	44
34.	Friday Morning News	45
35.	One Goal	47
36.	A Death in California	48
37.	Saint Patrick Over the Centuries	50
38.	The Ties that Bind	52
39.	Thoughtless	54
40.	Daily Giving	55
41.	The Give & Take of It All	56
42.	Sugar Bowl Napkin	57

SONGS

43.	Baby Boy	58
44.	Lee's Song	59
45.	Sweet Marie	60
46.	In Out Time Together	61
47.	Makes Life Richer	62
48.	Let's Bank on Love	63

PRAYERS

49.	Thanksgiving Prayer	64
50.	Prayer #1	65
51.	Prayer #2	66

POEMS

52.	Cruising the Danube	67
53.	Formula	68

INTRODUCTION

The purpose of this book is to share some of my writings from the last forty-five years. Although I started out to be a writer, I found that teaching took up more and more of my time and energy, and paid the bills, and was to become my main working contribution in our society. Once I accepted the fact that I was here to be a teacher, I came to very much enjoy the process and experience.

Over the years I taught more than five thousand high school students in the Acalanes Union High School District of Lafayette, California, and over a thousand secondary teachers earning their teaching credentials at the satellite campus in Walnut Creek of Chapman University. I never did let the writing totally go away, and it moved from front to back burner to pilot light and around the flame level of the stovetop. I continue to write monthly for our local newspaper the Orinda News as an education staff writer, as well as regularly in my journals, and now have the opportunity to publish this book of poems, songs and prayers.

The poems generally proceed from early to recent. I created most of the poems from my regular journal writing, but some I wrote for special occasions: Your Life Flowing for the baccalaureate speech I gave for a graduating class of Campolindo High School in Moraga, CA; The MLK poem from a poetry class I taught at St. Mary's High School in Oakland, California where the students and I read our poems to an assembly of parents; the Saint Patrick Over the Years a commission from my editor of the Orinda News for the March 2013 issue; 1981 Re-Visited was a poem I wrote at the request of the

San Francisco Channel 4 News team doing a story on my writing which ran on the 5pm news show on Christmas Day of 1981. That performance where I read the poem aloud with background video current events news scenes running along with classical music playing can be seen on my web site: obcustomverse.com. I wrote others on envelopes, napkins or any handy piece of paper

The Unconscious Streams series I wrote over a period of a month many years ago as an experiment. Daily upon awaking, I immediately picked up my journal and pencil and wrote as rapidly as possible without thinking about or paying attention to what I was saying, just trying to pour out in words what was in my subconscious. I edited these to make them slightly more coherent.

Some people would argue that poetry is more popular than ever in America today, but I maintain, to say the least, that poetry is not popular in our society; or more accurately, it doesn't sell. And when was the last time you read a poem in a newspaper, magazine or heard one read aloud on the radio or television? (The occasionally intelligible poem in the *New Yorker* excepted, of course. And, thank you Garrison Keillor for the *Writer's Almanac*.) I would like to suggest that since most people do not read poetry regularly that there are several ways to proceed with this book, in addition to the usual linear method: Read several poems in one sitting, in any order; or read one per day, or one per week – and take a year to read the book. In other words, read them your own way, at your own pace. Each poem is its own story.

I hope at the very least, one or more of these poems rings a bell, touches a nerve, releases some feeling or provokes a thought, giving the reader something to ponder, as we proceed living on this most magnificent and mysterious planet, filled with love and pain, and everything in between, dealt out in doses and torrents, cultivated and grown wild, in ceaseless individual and group dramas, on a ball in space that appears to be still, but is spinning at just over 1,000 miles an hour and coursing through its orbit around the sun at nearly 67,000 miles an hour.

A HAPPY DAY

One day beneath the trees
I saw the age of earth,
Wrinkled on a lady's face
Above her cane beyond her birth.

A glint of light sparked
Joy from her eyes smiling,
The day of a Renaissance Faire
Of happiness everywhere.

As daily in the sun
Somewhere in everyone,
The same light streams
In and out of every dream.

BILL O'BRIAN

EXTENSIONS OF THE SUN

When we begin
To touch
Inside each other,

We reach
More
Than we know.

Like a mountain stream
Filling
A dark pool silent,

This touch begins
To star
The night clear.

HUMANS BEING

We are
        Our own
                Limitations,

In
        No
                End,

        Of Longing. . . . .

BILL O'BRIAN

WHERE YOU STAY

The same burden remains alive unlike history,
To open those weighted doors that hold us
In harmony, discord, stasis, resolution,
Giving no clue to their unseen birth.

Who happens to stumble upon himself,
Needs no mirror to light cellar hallways
Hiding secrets of pleasure and pain,
Has indeed found a self of sorts
In surrounding streams and rain,

And need not wait for anybody else
To smile and lead the way,
For no matter where you are,
You are only where you stay.

INSIDE AS USUAL

The radio just said NASA is running tests
To see if man can withstand the isolation of the moon.

I laughed shaking my head when it is all you can do here
To withstand the isolation of being.

BILL O'BRIAN

MATTERS BETWEEN

As the moon minds its balance,
And the sun waves warm to the growth,
This planet's people pull the light of stars
Around their eyes, blinded by it,
Or its servant in the night.

Lovers' tongues lick the luck of time,
And can live that moment forever.
And fear flocks to fright like huddling monkeys,
Wearing knowing furtive grins, feeding each
Other the sacred hatred meat of who's the enemy.

LISTEN TO THE SPIRIT

If you haven't stopped talking
About what is holding us down,

It will be difficult to hear
What is calling us up,

Often as silently
As shadows dance.

BILL O'BRIAN

OPTIONS/ACTIONS

Twen   tieth

Zen   Jury

Tech   no

Logic

Pro   cess

Of   be

Ing,

More   or

Less   you

Man.

Chances   are

Chances   to

Be,

More   or

Less   hue

Man.

20th ZEN JURY

BE HERE NOW

Any message
I could
Bring

Has already
Been
delivered.

As easily
As you could
Dig these words,

You could be
Enjoying the sun,
Trees, or yourself

Being,
Your own
Poem.

BILL O'BRIAN

SHORTY

"Now going to the moon,
I can see it once.

I mean we found out,
Lets say,
It ain't no gold mine."

UNCONSCIOUS STREAMS #1

Like stumbling down corridors of lost suns,
Birds fly black through ambushes of evil wind,

And cat eyes look up stretching into nothing.
The earth turns, stars burn,

And people pull patterns of confusion within harmony
Like plastic man all around themselves entwined.

All the laws are working all the time,
People living less colors born to be diminished.

Dying doesn't determine destiny;
Death's dealer does; we wish wait worry wonder

> Like bird glides
> Like trees burning
> Like lovers lost
> Like silver bleeding
> Like farms fresh.

Whoever dares demands destinies,
Bushes bleak baring souls, whispering trees moving
With wind unseen itself, fog floating skies of ecstasy;

BILL O'BRIAN

There are no destinies only demands demanding to be filled
And white blossoms burst to blackness in silence.

The lone remaining star from night holds its peace together;
The night lights still shine unknown to morning.

Easing color of light blue
Through a pale shade of gold to hill blackness,

Like white smoke clouds floating into skies disappearing
Like silver dragons flying in some memory of burning,

Birds barking like dogs; people crying like cats,
The sun spinning crazily through the sky

With flashes of night bursting like exploding tears,
Only long enough to scare the people poor from faith
Into noticing their heart pumping blood in the same

Motion of silence, smoothness, beauty,
Of inevitable birth growth dissolution,

Feeling people designs remaining,
Working as initiated in skies of meaning.

UNCONSCIOUS STREAMS #3

Longing to be living dance on beaches of imagined pleasures,
Postponing black questions to the sorrow of remembering,
The animals aren't lost just living instinct.

Oceans open air breathing upon land, trees rise and run
Laughing into tears flowing seasons of sweet fruit.

People questions pull for planets to fill fully,
But skies hold their own secrets,

Of changing color and stormy gifts of growth,
Worming home to the sun unknown to beauty,

Like wine wasted, water not tasted,
Like loving laughed at, like lost.

For worries white as clouds crumbling
Stand on the edge of pain feeling more

Insane washed and wasted who only
Can be felt for and helped none,

BILL O'BRIAN

Because understanding long sailed
Beneath winds of unseen meaning,

Past the kings of colors
Past a kind word alone into the night of living,

Pleasing to be filled with some form
Of anything, to make meaning more than nothing,

As flickering mothers bear sons carrying
Burdons of unresolved emptiness and loss

Leaving cracked crayon dreams crying tears
In confusion of misuse and sadness lingers,

Like heavy skies fogged gray filling minds,
And I think no energy will be wasted,

Nothing lost like no death for dying,
Serving birth like a welcome to the dawn.

UNCONSCIOUS STREAMS #4

Fading darkness allows embarkation
To bring the gifts of ages,

Dreams of seen schemes plucked from timeless
Experience and imagination of winds lacking,

Like wishing and wondering around humans past
Who were with one once, living now at least in dreams,

Like life of seeming possibility and symphonies
of longing sound,
Desires flying across the skies of dreaming,

Wrapping spidery webs around eyes too blind to see
Such misty threads of aiming like changing faces

Of places where marching men have stepped and swept
Whole vineyards into slabs of homes and businesses

Pumping up profits like balloons of banks,
So spinning for one reason or another

The planet holds us still to grow within
Like so many flowers of no purpose and

In this reason of growing, changes become beautiful,
Yet while the soundless sorrows weep rivers

BILL O'BRIAN

Of pain flooding forever in their source,
There is beauty in becoming stronger, leaving tears forgotten,

So depths of oceans heave and flow
Untouched, unseen like the mind of man,
And in our growing millions of years we too might see

The source of sorrow and fears, the gift of light,
The feel of love, the wanting to be more,
Becoming better days,

But they say the cycles are returning like fashions
And that seems no mystery when one thinks

Of all the circles surrounding us,
Seen again through our minds of past presence,

And a two year young child toddles around a restaurant
Talking to us all in babbling, touching our levels

In curiosity, smiles, beauty, and innocence bursting from
Her baby eyes, free to roam in love assured.

Disappearing noise trails shadows across the skies,
And birds sing to morning as always they have done.

UNCONSCIOUS STREAMS #5

The day is dark with rain from the gray clouds of season
Washing air of feeling; the birds call from wires
And sing to empty ears that are blank to roaring,

For the feeling of the trees alone hurts and reminds
Too much of mistakes made moving oblivious
To the song of nature like beasts of deep caves
That rage in silence at chains of restriction,

That unseen bind the mind to the mud of missed meaning
And the fog finds warning blowing through her color
To the pawns of peddling pleasure alone and unhappy,

All days one love night the jungle rhythms rock
The air as snapping, popping, bouncing bodies
Writhing through the feeling of vibrating rhythm
From wood and pounding drums in beats of air,

Entering people jumping to the essence of movement,
Of earth life born to the wilderness as basic believing
In the power of life in spaces empty of answers,

BILL O'BRIAN

So the birds are worshipped and respected for their songs
And little white buddhas are carved in ivory, and colors of light
Reflect off liquid reminding one of pearls, ebony, teak,

Redwood and jade which carry the character of star points
Shining distant wondering into the hearts of eyes,

That blink white liquid light and remain beyond speech
In respect of overflowing,

Living loving as calm words to soothe a rambling mind
Like sun warmth, soft scents of incense, jasmine,
Rose, magnolia blossom,

In silence in peace in knowing life a river
How to round a rock

Flowing, forward, completing circles to mend.

PROVERBS

Who prays to the spirit of seasons,
Accepts his place like a river.

Whose words hold down another,
Adds himself to the night.

Who imagines himself a rock,
Will fall with an avalanche.

Who places another before him,
Kisses the soul of all living.

Who carries his reverence before him,
Is himself the vessel of life.

Who sends his roots through the flesh of earth,
Returns with the light of the heavens.

Who seeks the health of the whole,
Understands all aspects of living.

BILL O'BRIAN

MISTER DOCTOR MARTIN LUTHER KING

Mister Doctor Martin Luther King, we remember you,
Remember your strength and peace, and the brightness
Of your dream, squarely facing the violence of men.

Brother of the poor, man of dreams,
We salute your strength and bow thankfully
For the life you lived for others, always before you.

Mister Man of possibility, harbinger of peace,
Your voice sang
With the weight and pain of the centuries.

I heard you speak one day in Sacramento,
And the feeling and depth your commitment rang forth
Brought chills up my spine.

And I knew you were a man of peace and power,
Of right and justice,
And the dream you prophesized
Was our souls growing.

Mister King of the common man,
Marching at the front
Of your people,
Walking peacefully forth,

Before the rocks and clubs and guns,
Where hatred streamed
Down the streets and gutters
With the blood and sadness of the wounds,

Mister King of dignity and pride,
Beauty and justice,
We remember you today,
And honor your strength of vision,

And the sacrifice your living gave
Each and everyone to show us,
The beauty of our souls.

BILL O'BRIAN

TO MY STUDENTS
To acquaint them with John Lennon's death December 11, 1980

Death is something that comes sneaking,
Up out of nowhere, and slams you
On the head, knocks you down
In disbelief, and tears you life apart…

Death is something that in silence,
Roars and screams at you
From the pain of sobbing tears,
Telling you life is out of your hands…

Death is something no one can bear,
And everyone must,
Telling you life is here and gone,
In an instant, like dust…

Death is something that is never easy;
It rips your life and love to smitherines,
Telling you in your body's pain,
Part of your life is dead and gone forever…

Memories become all you have,
Of the person who so filled your life,
Who gave to you and smiled with you,
Who is now a thought only, from receding past…

I say open your hearts to everyone near,
And live each moment as if a year;
Give and receive all you can;
Life is moving, through your fingers, like sand.

20th ZEN JURY

1981 REVISITED

The Home of the Brave this 81st year started with peaceful,
Quelled tears for prisoners of politics, returning as heroes
To a yellow ribbon covered home that remembered them,
The same home that had no ribbons for forgotten heroes
Of the earlier undeclared Asian war.

Presidents come and go and sooner or later we all know
Which is what kind of man as he takes his stand;
1981 in the Land of the Free began with a new possibility,
The other political side of the coin, the people's choice,
A businessman.

New beginnings, we've seen them before, and seen weapons
End them too, and sure enough, American as apple pie,
Bullets fly, a president is gunned down again, but like
Hollywood movies, he holds on to life, and walks
From the hospital, joking with nurses, life just like the movies.

Congress gets a lesson in how a president gets what he wants,
Unseen in Washington since the arm twisting days of LBJ,
Tax and budget cuts sail past Congress, like a rocket ship
Through clouds, unable to resist the personal charm
Of phone calls from the White House Man.

Baseball called out on strikes, splitting the season in two,
But tip your hat to the Dodgers doing what they had to do,
Cleaning the Yankee's clocks, knocking 'em out of their socks,
Right out the door in the final four, and with a rookie to boot.

BILL O'BRIAN

Television was Dallas, America's cowboy, rich man fantasy,
Intrigue super wealth dream; sly guy J.R., nasty as can be,
Always lands on his feet, and closer to life's meaning,
Ms. O'Conner, the first female Supreme Court Justice,
Brings the woman's mind and heart to shape the laws
      Of the land, at last.

Prices are up, jobs are down, and Reagan's plan has yet to work;
Even D. Stockman, the man with the economic plan, says
He doesn't know what the figures mean, but just ask any
Of the 8.4% unemployed, and they will tell you how
      Economics re-figures a person's life and plans.

Recession arrives at year's end with inflation still up,
Car sales down to the worst level in 20 years; picture shows
Devoid of crowds, though economists claim to know,
People can show bad going to worse, for jobs desperately needed
      Are not there, and people still are, and hungry too.

California's Med Fly crisis quarantines thousands of acres
Of fruit while the governor's man drinks a glass of the poison
To show it won't hurt you, and people clamor for the government
To release millions of pounds of cheese to give to the hungry,
      Which occurs amazingly enough.

And as shoppers rush to Christmas gifts, Glide Memorial Church
Gives gifts of food to needy people, in tune with the truest spirit
Of Christmas, and now is the time for us all to look upon
Our year of living, to see how much closer we can all be,
      To the spirit of giving.

      May the blessings of Christmas
      Be forever yours!

FREQUENT RESPONSES

Mind signals feel signals fate signals stereo flesh signals;
Frequencies—responses, tuning stations into people
Feeling more than only.

> Eyes spark, huddle in the dark,
> And dictates are received.

> Vision is a different frequency,
> Feeling beyond the eye and ear.

> Covering everything,
> Cars, clothes and houses
> Dominate reality.

> Dreams treated as disturbances,
> And people needing help
> from streets as fleas.

Beating down a path of people
Where an un-thought is thought to side,

> Beating down a path of self,
> Erupting nowhere to hide.

BILL O'BRIAN

Frequencies of responses,
Responses to frequencies.

Frequent responses
To different tunings of mind.

Frequent tuning changes
Lack reception, lightly
Touching outside feeling.

Frequency tuned into
Who is sending feeling
Down the time of flesh and air,

Responds with frequent believing,
Depth of feeling, people out there.

So many flooded receivers sending,
All these responses everywhere.

YOUR LIFE FLOWING

Starting high school a freshman is leery, concerned,
Startled at new prospects, the bigger people, all
So new and different; the move to high school
Is fearful, yet quickly full of life and faces and friends.

Becoming a stream of days and fears and tears
Turning to ways to grow and change and life moves
On into years and summers and studies, sports,
Dances, vacations, tests and a senior year approaching.

The long awaited senior year, the angst of SAT's over,
Speeding by in ball games, art projects, rallies, music
Practiced, played and marched, flags twirling,
The Senior Ball, a day in San Francisco, and here we are.

What should you do? Be alive in the present moment,
Honor yourself by honoring others, and all life, continue
The fine path you and your family and friends
Have been sculpting over the years.

Which bridge should you take? A bridge is a connection,
And they are everywhere, for better or worse; your
Attitude is your main bridge – it will set the tone and carry
You through your journey; your better judgment will choose

The best bridges to cross, to connect with people
And events; E.M. Forster said, "Only connect."
Meaning genuinely connect and create bridges
With others, with foundations from values beyond lifetimes.

BILL O'BRIAN

Life is learning, living and loving and growing, getting
Slammed with bad news and crawling back up to your feet.
Love is caring for others more than yourself, giving time
As proof you care, spirit revealing your self to the world.

The sun rises daily; the moon moves the tide in salt scented air.
The stars sparkle and beam points of light, and people dream.
Contradictions abound in the Yin and Yang, all around
Opposites reveal the other deep side of the coin.

Your life, your love, your growth is as important
As every moment living, and is yours to be giving
As others show you who you are, and your desires
Create the worlds to come, dreams that take root, then fly.

Good living is simple, deep, profound across the timeless ages,
Yet is playful and lighthearted like a child.
Knowing when to be serious, when to laugh, feeling
The darkness of pain, yet knowing happiness will prevail.

We learn to grow by going inside ourselves so we may
Take our gifts of accomplishment to the world; the spirit
Of life flows like a river of light, like the early rays of dawn,
In all the forms of ourselves to the material world.

As the daily golden sun rises may your own horizons grow.
May you learn to transcend by understanding
Others and your self,
Grow roots so wings can emerge, unfold
And your dreams take flight.
William Blake says, "No man flies too high on his own wings."

Live and love every second within the skies.
Kiss the moment as it flies.
Give and receive all you can.
Life is flowing—through your fingers—like sand.

ANOTHER MOMENT IN TIME
11/15/2001

Voices in the background,
Birds in the trees.
Bright sun is shining
Through baby blue,
In a light breeze.

A fine day, a Friday,
A warm November time,
Where teens chatter, birds
Blather, a moment of peace is mine.

The bell cuts the air;
Airplane engine patters away,
And the sun warms the day
As the breeze in the trees plays.

Just another flow of time,
A lunch break in the work day.
Peaceful background sounds
Soothe as the food my stay.

Teaching every day, showing
The path, methods, discipline,
Organized to say, the Cosmos
Cares to show roads to self and others.

BILL O'BRIAN

Lunchtime minutes
Of peaceful rest and food,
Quiet inside the natural flow
Of bird's and people's voices, I rest,
Then return to teach some more:

Macbeth, the mass murderer,
Fallen angel general,
So we can learn to rise ourselves,
Phoenixlike, from the daily ruin
Of our own lack of eyes.

LOVE IS THE DREAM

Love is the dream
Of the universe.
Love is the stream
Of our life.
Love takes us
Beyond the strife.

Love is the dream
Of all people.
Love is the stream
Of our fate.
Love takes us
To the heights.

Love is the dream
Of our Goddesses.
Love is the stream
Of all time.
Love takes us
To the lights.

BILL O'BRIAN

NOT A WORD BETWEEN THEM

Las Vegas Airport, Saturday, January 13, 2007,
Approximately 1:30 p.m. in a fast food restaurant:

I sit and eat my god knows what
Sauce laden spaghetti and meatballs
For lunch between planes.

At the next table sits a quintessential
Early 21st century American tech-no-logic family:
Father, teenage son, teenage daughter,
Linked 24-7 to a virtual world.

All three throughout the meal talk
On their own cellphones
To someone else, elsewhere.

The father leads the way with a constant low murmur,
Cell phone to his ear, messages of great import,
Beyond this time together with his children.

The son alternately folds, unfolds his phone,
Plays games, fiddles with buttons, talks to someone,
Answers calls from somewhere.

20th ZEN JURY

The daughter rests her dead down
Upon her arm already laying on the table,
Like a bored teenager in class, ready to sleep.

She chats and listens to someone beyond her family,
Her whole body showing tiredness and disinterest,
Beside her brother and father.

I finish my greasy red sauce laden
(really quite filling and satisfying)
Plate of spaghetti and meatballs.

I am done and leave them to their Marshall McLuhan
"Global Village", ceaseless interconnected
World of modern life.

Wondering what good is it all, if one cannot connect,
Face to face, person to person, father to children,
In moments together?

When one day all will be gone: their time together,
Their lives, their youth, their love, and their chance
To be alive together in a moment.

As a foundation of family, giving solace in pain,
Support in weakness, themselves to each other,
In all they only really have:

In the rolling years of their lives,
Just a little time together.

BILL O'BRIAN

SOME THOUGHTS FOR SHERYL & JERRY
06/12/2007

A mother's worst nightmare comes true to life,
And shatters her dreams in war torn strife.

She brings her baby into the world,
Loves, nurtures and raises him up to be a man,
Torn from earth in a bullet's flight.

All the loving, caring and tending
Comes crashing to an end.
The boy she knew to be a man,
Gave his life serving his land.

No words or tears or anything
Can relieve the pain of goodbye.
Only time incessant day and night
Will ever reveal any peace or light.

Torn from his mother and father,
A lightning bolt of pain
Rips the heart and love so full.
Now only grief surrounds, remains.

20th ZEN JURY

Old age and years of living given come to a natural end,
But when the young and healthy go,
A garden of grief is left to tend.
When youth so strong and bright are gone,
Only pain remains, the dying of the light.

They say time heals all wounds, but these are feckless words,
And time will tell its tale of who can reveal
A heaven from a living hell.

We are born; we grow, we live, we die.
We do the best we can.
No beauty is revealed without its companion opposite side.

So all one can do is just get through,
And pray we live to see and be,
The heaven we know is deep inside,
The essence of life, the soul of eternity.

BILL O'BRIAN

THE SOULFUL VAN SINGS OF PAIN

I hear the man and those in his band,
Sing with the spirit of our Irish soul.

His soul full sound brings my tears
Up and down, from all the years.

He sings the sound of ancient pain,
Streaming right to my soul, through my veins.

I drop the worn leather gloves on the deck,
Take a work break, for the pen, the soul's sake.

The timeless pain flows through me, around,
Brings up tears for all, endless memory abounds.

I sit and take a short
Shot of whiskey,

And toast all the pain
God gave us,

And toast all the men,
And women, who help save us.

KEEPING FAITH IN MIND

Take a good thing; bring it around.
Do a little too much; run it in the ground.

Start out slowly; gain some speed.
First, it's fun; now, it's a need.

Take anything: T.V., credit cards,
Smoking, sex; have a little, then a lot.

You take a little pleasure, then too much.
Now, you gotta have it; soon, you're out of touch.

Ah, the addictions to sensual life! How they morph!
From delight, to sinking, struggling, grappling plight!

What to do?
Clean house—body, mind and soul.

Faith in mind over matter,
The only strength to make the soul whole.

BILL O'BRIAN

OUR FRIEND INDEED

I've got a good old friend I've known since children play.
I'm going to see him soon while he's here another day.

Friends in childhood, teens on teams,
College pranks, chasing beauties down the streams.

Years go beyond friends, the closest remain,
Keeping us together, our memories all the same.

Wives and children come and grow; we live, we work,
We care; we share all that we know.

And life moves on within us and without us,
Taking us together down the road of living time.

And then the day arrives, time to say the last goodbye.
Our friend departs this world, and we feel the empty space.

Time no longer filled with friendship tilled.
Gone are the days we roamed and played.

Gone is the time life flowed like wine.
Hello, goodbye, to our dearest friend.

You made our lives worth all the living, right down to the end.
A man for all seasons, a man for all people,

Interested in you, interesting to hear,
He could talk with anyone, and they all felt near.

FROM MAY TO JUNE
05/03/2006

Spring's here; summer's near.
Let our smiles be our cheer.
Let's buckle down, get it done,
Whether hot or clouded sun.

Let not the teens of temptation talk,
Where they beg we do not run but walk.
Let our natural smiles and cheer,
Reveal the value of each moment near.

So on we go, quotidian flow,
Digging into wisdom we all know.
The moment flies as it arrives,
And we kiss infinity in the skies.

BILL O'BRIAN

GOLF ON A SUNNY AFTERNOON

Golf on a sunny afternoon makes us feel better than a silver spoon.
Taking a break to play makes us feel now is a civilized day.

    Blue skies, cut green grass, sculpted earth and sunshine
    Take a woman's spirit and whisper, "You lucky lass."
    Friends, companions, compatriots all taking a little time
    From the daily grind, to stroll, swing and chat; that's all.

Drive the ball high and long, then muff it; what went wrong?
Appreciating each other's strokes, encouraging, enjoyable folks.
Fairway shots beautiful, some doggonit in the rough.
Sun and grass surround; life's not so tough.

Pitch and chip, in sand and out, light of sun on land in sheen.
We walk together, all five balls, waiting, still, upon the green.
Putts are long and close, but miss; some surprise, drop down in.
Many inch closer, too short, too long; some look good, a win.

To the clubhouse reward, chilled beer, glasses clink, refreshing
Good fortune, earned and flowing; we're here.
Relaxing in chairs, sipping cold tea; love those fries!
All happy eyes, satisfied, chit chat, share news, way past the blues.

Another day, another dollar; we did our work, then loosened collar.
Played our game, about the same; we will return another day.
Refresh our friendships, relax, recreate the game,
And ourselves, together an oasis in the world, untaxed.

    The unseen cycle spins the earth,
    Each day's sun and moon a brand new birth.
    Clear skies, another afternoon, golf and friends;
    How wonderful! And none too soon!

SUMMER'S HERE; LET'S CHEER!

Take some time
From the daily grind.
Renew, refresh, recreate
Idling engines of the mind.
Relax, reshape, regroup,
Together get it back:
On a summer day
Childhood play.

Take a break
From the daily grind.
Take a breath of fresh air.
Take your own sweet time.
One life to live; one life to give.
Renew and age yourself
Inside the flow of life,
Like a fine wine.

GOOD TO GO

When you're groovin' with day,
You've got something to say, sharing
In every way—you're good to go;
You're in the know.

When you're skipping down the street,
You're feeling neat, picking up others
In your beat—you're good to go;
You're good to show.

When you share that smile,
Bust beyond your trials, giving someone
Help along the mile—you're good to go;
Along the row you hoe.

When you reach out from within,
Your soul taps beyond the grin, helping others
Daily win—you're good to go;
Let 'em know:

All the souls of Heaven and Earth
Share the same Divine Birth,
As each learns, assists the other,
Like the Divine Child,
Divine Father
and
Divine Mother Earth.

CHRISTMAS EVE

Keep it simple.
Keep it clean.
Go for happy.
Forget the mean.

Think love.
Think beauty.
Receive those gifts
Timeless from above.

So many people
Want life so right.
They live; they die.
They're looking for
The light,

Of a moment,
For an hour,
Just the comfort,
Like the view,
From a tower.

Confidence,
Assurance,
A kind word
In the night;

Sometimes,
That's all it takes,
To make someone's
Day just right.

BILL O'BRIAN

LOOK AROUND

Worlds are filled
With people's needs;
Love is giving
Time in deeds.

20th ZEN JURY

FRIDAY MORNING NEWS

As each does to oneself, one does to another.
The love one leaves outside oneself, does not stray, but hovers.

The weakness one shows to the world at large
Reveals an inside lack of charge.

Easy ways cannot stay; no roots are temporary stays.
Patterns show a quick fix lacks hope, faith and glow.

As one does to another, one does to self;
Karma is the name.

Until conditions allow the mind's desire to choose,
One trap remains in all the games:

The strengths of habit wrap themselves around
Any hope to unbound.

Only when circumstance declares no other chance,
Will change begin to grow.

For all must learn to live and learn,
Or destroy the gift of blessed life.

No one can do for another what must be done by self.
For all must be the single light of we.

BILL O'BRIAN

All good things come from within, take time, develop
In discipline, in choices freedom brings.

One can hope; one can pray.
One can show another all the love that cares.

But on this earth each must stand alone as tall,
Or fall to the failure within:

The self serving isolation of one moment's pleasure,
After another, until the goddesses cease to tend,

The death of life, the loss of love, weakness triumphs,
Right down to the end, just around the bend.

But one thing remains at the bottom in Pandora's Box,
Holds all the keys, dreams and doors one will ever need.

Hope is there, and always will be.
One must awaken enough to see
The beauty of the sun on the morning trees,

And the love of those so near,
Who always were most caring
In the hour of one's greatest need.

20th ZEN JURY

ONE GOAL

Minimum needs.
Maximum deeds.

BILL O'BRIAN

A DEATH IN CALIFORNIA

Even Hospice ceased to show.
They said he was too mean,
For them to help him,
Let himself go.

Not in the door,
Not any more,
Not after what he says;
He can die alone.

I am sorry;
There are limits to caring:
Insults, nastiness,
Meanness to the end.

All he does is yell vilely
As if others are to blame
For his wretched state
Of mind and bodily plight.

There were always choices;
He made his.
Then his children left,
Never re-entering the door.

Baseness overtook him;
Spite and blame grew like flame.
His center of selfishness
Filled the room.

Fighting to the end with those
Who came to help and care,
Spitting venom to those
Who love and share.

He dies a nasty, wicked old man,
After all the choices
Creation spread across
His daily, mostly sunny land.

He took his anger, embodied it in his soul,
Left the love alone that could make him whole.
Nothing was good enough,
For this wretched, spleenful old man.

In the end it was all about him.
He missed the boat.
It sailed without him filled with people
Who tried to help him cope.

He chose his path and blamed those
Who finally left him alone,
Facing his death in life, disowned,
Angry, mean, too selfish to glean

The glow of love burning in the night
From people weaned on light,
Who had to step aside and let him be
Swallowed by his own, vicious, black tide.

BILL O'BRIAN

SAINT PATRICK OVER THE CENTURIES

The brutal Irish slave raiders arrived at night
to England,
From the black, dark sea, from leather boats,
armed in pain
To snatch the teenage boy Patricius
from his Roman home,
Off and away from his family, and the heart
of his parents.

Taken to the misty hills of Ireland to live
alone, cold, hungry,
Tending sheep for his master Miliucc,
the warrior chief,
He learned to survive, giving constant
prayers day and night,
To the God of his parents who were long
gone from his life.

Six years of "woeful isolation" transformed him
from man to Holy Man,
Who heard a mystery voice say,
"Your hungers are rewarded;
You are going home." Awaking from sleep,
again it said, "Look,
Your ship is ready." Knowing not where
he was, or was to go, he left.

Walking 200 miles until he found the sea,
the bay, the ship, his goal,
He cajoled to board, telling the crew,
"I come in God's strength."
They said, "Come aboard, we trust you."
And they sailed to Gaul.
Arriving to land ruined by war, they starved,
walking for two weeks.

20th ZEN JURY

Finally, Patricius says, "Trust the Lord;
you will have food today."
The sailors pray, and stampeding sounds
of pig hooves fill the air,
Food at last, for their bodies, for their faith,
for their belief in Patricius.
In a monastery, he becomes the first
Christian bishop missionary ever.

Returning to Ireland after a visit to his parents
who begged him to stay,
He changes the Emerald Isle to Christian belief
becoming its Patron Saint,
Creating bishoprics from Ullster to Tara to Meath;
adding monasteries and convents,
slavery died, violence decreased,
and God's love grew.

His legacy lives today as people of the world
from Argentina to Russia,
New Zealand to South Korea, Japan and Canada
all celebrate together,
With world churches from Catholics
to Eastern Orthodox to Lutheran,
Honor as one, The Feast of St. Patrick,
the day he died, March 17, 461.

St. Patrick carried God's love to the land
of the Irish,
And it unceasingly grew throughout
the world wherever
Irish live to love the life God gave them.
He convinced them.
God's love would save them, in this world
and the next.

BILL O'BRIAN

THE TIES THAT BIND

The ties that bind
Will one day
Make you cry.

To feel that love
You will one day
Say goodbye.

Love is here to give.
Love is here to live.
But one day all
Must say goodbye.

The smiles come and go.
The tears will someday show,
How you felt, what you gave,
And what you now know.

Love has come to you,
And you had time to renew,
Feelings for another,
The same love given you.

What one can feel
Is love made real.
What one can gain
Goes beyond pain.

The ties that bind
That made you sigh,
Will unravel to the sky.

The ties that bind
Will one day
Make you cry.

THOUGHTLESS

In our marriage,
She is the other
Half of me.

What I say
And do to her,
I do to myself.

For better or worse.

DAILY GIVING

I have been given
A beautiful wife.
She has given me
Her entire life.

How can I honor
Such love for me?

By being all
I can see and be,
For her, for us,
For all our parents
Ever dreamed.

By daily giving
To her, more
Than I have
Been given,
If that is possible,
Than what she
Has given me.

BILL O'BRIAN

THE GIVE & TAKE OF IT ALL

Take to Survive;
Give to Thrive.

SUGAR BOWL NAPKIN
03/20/2014

Air of blue
Mountains white,
As seasons change,
Stand still
As light.

BABY BOY

I left my baby boy crying today.
He saw his daddy leaving; I didn't know he felt that way.

I had to leave as I went to work.
It made me sad, but my ego did perk.

Chorus:
I felt so good he wanted me today.
I'm keeping him tomorrow, and we'll stay and play.

I love the little boy with all my heart.
The beauty of his mother gave us both her spark.

I'll tell you now as I'm coming home,
I hope your spirit soars to roam.

Chorus:
I felt so good he wanted me today.
I'm keeping him tomorrow, and we'll stay and play.

LEE'S SONG

Oh Lord, I say, You gave me a scare,
Something I do not want to think about.

You gave me the fear that loosens all of my tears.
Lord, I do not want to have to cry and shout.

Chorus:
This love I know, You gave us to show,
The beauty and the fullness of Your tide.
Oh, my baby boy, I thank You for his love and joy.
I tell you, Lord, he's one I do not want to live without.

I just want to be alive
And growing like a big oak tree,
And show you, Lord, I can tend my family.

The silver glint in the morning sun
Is streaming gold down the blue of his early run,
High above my boy and I who are so happy today.

Chorus:
This love I know, You gave us to show,
The beauty and the fullness of Your tide.
Oh, my baby boy, I thank You for his love and joy.
I tell you, Lord, he's one I do not want to live without.

BILL O'BRIAN

SWEET MARIE

Sweet Marie, little Ah Hee,
Sweet Marie, our Ah Hee,
Sweet Marie, lovely Ah Hee,
You've come to join our love, our family.
You've come to join our love, our family.

Chorus:
You came happy into our lives,
Open arms, gift of the skies.
You bring gentleness into our eyes.
I am so happy we are alive.
I am so happy love fills our sky.

Sweet Marie, peaceful Ah Hee,
You came flying over the sea.
You bring your Asian beauty.
Sweet Marie, love is thee.
You complete our family.

Sweet Marie, smiling Ah Hee,
Sweet Marie, gentle Ah Hee,
Sweet Marie, peaceful Ah Hee,
I love your dark-eyed Asian beauty.
I love your dark-eyed Asian beauty.

Chorus:
You came happy into our lives,
Open arms, gift of the skies.
You bring gentleness into our eyes.
I am so happy we are alive.
I am so happy love fills our sky.

IN OUT TIME TOGETHER

When I say I love you, I know it's true.
When I say I love you, I know it's right.

When I say I care for you, I know it's true.
I want to show each day, time for you is right.

Chorus:
In our time together, we have sculpted a fine life.
We have grown so much greater than just man and wife.

When I say I need you, I know it's true.
You are the other half of me; your love is out of sight.

When I say I love you, I know it's true.
This love you always give, surrounds us all in light.

Chorus:
In our time together, we have sculpted a fine life.
We have grown so much greater than just man and wife.

When I say I care for you, I know it's true.
I just want to make your day so right.

When I say I love you, I hope you know it's true.
I just want to give you peace beyond the night.

Chorus:
In our time together, we have sculpted a fine life.
We have grown so much greater than just man and wife.

BILL O'BRIAN

MAKES LIFE RICHER

Look at that girl with the red dress on.
Look at the sweetheart dancing to my song.
Look at that lovely with the red dress on.
I bet she can boogie all night long.

Chorus:
Let her dance; let her prance;
Let her be herself; she's all you,
All you ever, ever dreamed.

Look at that lady, her swinging soul.
I bet she can make, make your life whole.
Take the lady into your heart.
Give both of you a brand new start.

Chorus:
Let her dance; let her prance;
Let her be herself; she's all you,
All you ever, ever need.

Take the lovely into your soul.
Together you can make each other whole.
Stop the silence, loneliness alone.
Live for each other, to each his own.

Makes life richer, something to share.
Give to one another all that you care.

Chorus:
Let her dance; let her prance;
Let her be herself; she's all you,
All you ever, ever dreamed.

LET'S BANK ON LOVE

We have a good thing going; let's not let it fall.
Let's bank on love, and we'll both stand tall.

We've had our blows on the roads and rocks of life.
Let's bet our love takes us, way beyond the strife.

Chorus:
Your love, my love, let's roll the dice.
The open road's the future, and your love,
Your love is, your love is so, nice.

We have a future and a dream for two.
Let's bet our love will both of us renew.

Your baggage, my past, we can let it go.
We have a bond; this we both do know.

Let bygones be gone; let the future unfold.
Let's pledge each other, new is better than the old.

Chorus:
Your love, my love, let's roll the dice.
The open road's the future, and your love,
Your love is, your love is so, nice.

BILL O'BRIAN

THANKSGIVING PRAYER

Dear Creator and Giver of Life,
We say thank You for the blessings,
You bestow upon us daily:
Family, love, health and happiness,
Allowing us productive lives to live.
Let us make our parents proud,
And our children the hope
Of tomorrow.

ThanksGiving Day
November, 28, 2002
Majors–O'Brian Dinner

PRAYER #1

May each person one and all,
Daily see the best within themselves,
Letting Your Love shine through
Their thoughts, words and deeds.
May each person exceed in giving
The love once given them by another,
So timeless Love continues,
Shown, shared and given,
Growing in the hearts of all
The souls on all the earth.

PRAYER #2

Dear Lord, may I be worthy of Your love
For me, my family and Your people of the earth.

May my thoughts reflect the highest and purest
Love as do Your thoughts for us.

May my words be clear and incisive,
Showing understanding and infinite love.

May my deeds be the best possible always,
For the benefit of all people everywhere,
Revealing what You wish for everyone.

May my prayers go from Your heart,
Through my heart to the hearts
Of all people everywhere.

So everyone on earth may experience,
The love and blessings You ceaselessly
Bestow upon us all.

CRUISING THE DANUBE

Life is passing by
Like the riverside,
Up and down the stream.

Life is passing by
Like the riverside,
In and out of every dream.

What is real is a bigger deal.
What is unreal is in your mind.

What you chose,
What you lose,
What you're fishing for,
In time.

BILL O'BRIAN

FORMULA

Grow wise with the ages,
And live young like a child.
Let your mind hold the reins,
As your imagination runs wild.

Bill O'Brian will write
a custom poem for you!

Ideal for:

• *Any Special Person or Occasion*
• *Anniversaries, Birthdays, Retirements*
• *Reunions and Family Histories*

For details, visit:
obcustomverse.com

www.ingramcontent.com/pod-product-compliance
Lightning Source LLC
Chambersburg PA
CBHW061341040426
42444CB00011B/3025